"The kind of liberation and voice that comes f
and mastery of one's own experience."

Ray Pillid
Adc

"Sue Harris is a marvel – she's engaging, thoughtful, funny and wise. And all those adjectives describe her new book, too. Need I say more?"
Adam Pertman
Executive Director of the Donaldson Adoption Institute
Author of *Adoption Nation*

"I have had the honor to hear all of Ms. Harris O'Connor's narratives, as well as to work beside her in connecting her words to action for social workers and parents. As an adoptive parent and child welfare professional, I have used her pieces to improve both supporting my children and performing my job. Everyone should read these important works, regardless of their connection – or not – to adoption. They open a door to better understanding ourselves and others in a way that I have not experienced before."
Kim Stevens, M.Ed.
Program Manager at the North American Council on Adoptable Children

"Having had the privilege to hear several of Sue's narratives, I have been impressed and touched by the pain yet humor, the depth yet hope her stories tell. She speaks the truth with rhythm and beauty."
Mathieu Bermingham, M.D.
Assistant Professor of Child and Adolescent Psychiatry
UMass Medical School

"As a transracial adoptee and adoption professional, Susan's narratives are essential because they recognize that one's identity is both emotional and cognitive in nature. The central question to her work is, 'How do we use the privilege we hold to either open or close doors of opportunity and understanding?' Through qualitative story sharing, Susan helps all members of the triad, and our allies, find the living and breathing answers to this crucial question."
Tara Linh Leaman, JD
Co-Founder and Vice-President, AmerAsians Building Bridges, and transethnic adoptee

"Susan Harris O'Connor is my dear friend and colleague of twenty years. We had the privilege to consult with one another, share our professional adoption experiences and travel with the Pre and Post Adoption consulting team in Somerville, MA to present at various conferences and trainings. As a result, we shared many personal moments and professional insights together. Susan has a uniquely profound, realistic understanding of the life-long complexities and connections for all those whose lives are touched by adoption. Susan has created and presented her dramatic narratives to thousands who have been enlightened, inspired and moved to laughter and tears. This book, The Harris Narratives, will be a gift to all who read it."

Sheridan Dana Robbins, LCSW
Birthmother/ Adoptive Mom/ Adoptee

"Many people are described as "originals," but Sue Harris is the genuine article. Her work has a unique freshness and crisp clarity to it that provokes both deep reflection and childlike playfulness. You will not read her book without having many stunning "AHA" moments and you will want to savor them again and again."

Sue Badeau
National Writer and Speaker on Childhood Trauma, Foster Care and Adoption

"Few people dig as deep into their own experience as Sue Harris O'Connor. (Few have to.) And nobody else comes back with these lyrical raucous stories that teach a thing or two. Or forget all that. The way Sue's storytelling combines spirit with intelligence with art just always blows me away."

Penny Callan Partridge
Poet

"The Harris's intensely personal life's narratives are both unique and universal to many of the poignancies of adoption. As someone who was adopted transracially and internationally as a child, Harris's narratives profoundly resonate with many of my own experiences and have contributed to a deeper understanding of my own personal journey and to my work as a psychotherapist with individuals who are often in search of the "self"."

Eileen Thompson, MSW, LICSW
Director, Wheelock College Counseling Center
Past Advisor, Tufts University Korean Student Association's
Big Brother/Sister Program for Korean Adopted Children
Establishing and Former Board Member, Boston Korean Adoptee's, Inc.
Private Practice, Greater Boston Area

"Susan Harris O'Connor, in her evolutionary narratives by which she worked on her personal identity issues from a complicated blend of cultures and origins, has created fascinating constructs which helped her survive, and will aid others as well. To first read them, then hear her present them has been instructive in understanding transracial adopted individuals. But, try to hear her present them. Unbelievable!"

Linda Clausen, MSW, LGSW
Coordinator, DCMETRO Concerned United Birthparents
Region 1 Director CUB
DC/MD State Rep. American Adoption Congress
Founder, ACCESS MARYLAND

"Sue Harris has taken the universal "search for self" and, through sharing with us her own inner experience, she teaches us how to take the journey for ourselves. Sue models for us how to illuminate the inner recesses of self, and in doing so, she leads the way for us all. Thank you, Sue, for this sacred gift."

Leah C. O'Leary, LICSW
Executive Director
A Red Thread Adoption Services, Inc.

"The revelations abound. As the second generation 'natural' son of White Irish immigrants, my 'box' was fairly simple and straightforward, or so I thought. The Harris Racial Identity Theory and its 5 constructs radically changed the prism through which I looked. Although far from a trans-racial adoptee - and even initially comforted by the simplicity of my own constructs - knowledge of the 5 constructs began to seep in and permeate my personal awareness and then my professional interactions. Diversity and inclusion now take on new richness and depth; the tapestry is much more colorful; the texture of diverse thought is much more palpable. Awareness and understanding of the constructs at work, coupled with balance and context of their impact in interpersonal relations, simply improves the social dynamic in many arenas. Sue's "Reflections" are as relevant in my occasionally staid corporate environment as they are in the halls of academia in opening up the lens through which we all see. Thank you Sue, for the tremendous insight."

Charlie O'Connor, SVP & Manager
Liberty Mutual Insurance | Commercial Insurance Claims

THE HARRIS NARRATIVES

An Introspective Study of a Transracial Adoptee

Susan Harris O'Connor

"One of the fundamental skills we try to teach emerging social work practitioners involves the capacity to turn, find, face, and embrace humanity in the other. This is very difficult to do for many reasons, one of which is related to the fear of having a truly authentic dialogue. Authenticity requires us to come to the table - naked and without shame. This is the invaluable gift Sue has given to all of us in this collection - the gift of authenticity of discourse so that we can all be transformed as a result."

Tien Ung, PhD, LICSW
Assistant Professor, Simmons School of Social Work

Published by The Pumping Station
61 Cleveland Street #2, Arlington, MA 02474-6935, USA
thepumpingstation.org

Online purchasers of this book who have not paid sales tax in their own jurisdiction (bit.ly/SalesTaxRates) should file use tax returns to report the purchase.

Library of Congress Cataloging-in-Publication Data

The Harris narratives: an introspective study of a transracial adoptee
/ Susan Harris O'Connor

    p. cm.

    Includes bibliographical references.

Library of Congress Control Number: 2012921486

ISBN   978-0-9849216-2-1 (pbk) 978-0-9849216-3-8 (cloth)
           978-0-9849216-4-5 (ebook)

FIRST EDITION
Printed by Lightning Source

For my beloved mother, the late Dorothea Rae Harris

1917-1989

and my beloved father, the late Dr. Samuel Nahum Harris

1922-1994

Your love continues on in all your children.

Table Of Contents

Preface

People write for different reasons. My writing began as a tool to assist me with my fear of public speaking. My inability to complete sentences or a train of thought when publicly interacting with scholars and professionals felt so pronounced, that I knew that I was either going to limit the scope of my professional endeavors, or step up and attempt to address my fears and what appeared to be my severe limitations.

I know that there are different styles and types of writing; I am not sure exactly what style or type mine is. Regardless, I can tell you that initially, my writings were not written by the love to write, or to showcase a competency at writing well-written sentences. My works were written slowly, over long periods of time and with great difficulty. Each word was positioned by emotions that were closely overseen by my clinical insights. Honestly, I've never been sure about sentence structure, proper grammar or other things that one is supposed to have learned in school. I didn't do well in that area. What has been important to me is the overall integrity of my work, which for me has very little to do with commas, sentence structure, or the usage of 'big' words. Integrity is about the picture that is painted. Does my work honor and accurately convey my true-life experience as a human being? Does it authentically honor a transracial adoptee's experience?

There is something humbling when you become aware of your shortcomings. Because of mine, I have a weak spot when I encounter people who never went further in their academic pursuits or careers because they didn't think they could do it, because they didn't score well, because they felt or were made to believe they were dumb. I get it!

However, I am amazed by the power of emotions and thoughts. I now know that they can turn a non-writer into a writer, that they can make a person who early on has no interest in developing a career or fighting for causes, become an educator and activist; that they can help an emotionally and psychologically injured person heal.

When I think about how I arrived at this place today, two people stand out. My mother, my adoptive mother who was a graduate of the Girls Latin Exam School and who graduated with a degree in chemistry from Jackson College, which is now known as Tufts University, never gave up on me, forcing me to read and write throughout the years. I can still hear her attempting to explain to me how to write a sentence, what goes into a paragraph, and what makes for a good introduction. My mother, a woman who would be 95 years old today if she were alive, raised six kids, two of whom scored perfect SAT scores. And one of whom she taught two years of Latin over the course of a summer to assist while at Groton. But she had her greatest challenges when it came to teaching me. I know she left this world slightly concerned about whether I would survive as a professional because she understood that I had never mastered writing simple sentences. I think that I was actually puzzling to her.

My birth mother or, as some might refer to her, my first mother, whom I found immediately following the death of my mother in 1990, is the second person that comes to mind. During the first of many very lengthy conversations with her, I learned that she had been double-promoted in high school, entered Brandeis University at the age of 16, and was among the first graduating classes of that institution. She was a known artist in the Bay Area, an art professor in San Francisco, a published author, and an expert on copyright for artists. I was actually rather shocked to learn how talented and smart she was.

From this relationship, I began to contextualize more about my situation. I had grown up during a time, within a geographical location, and within a family structure, where the traditional teaching and standardized testing that worked for many, because it reinforced something that they did well, didn't work for me. Being around my birth mother made it clear that there are many ways of expressing one's understanding and aptitude that can't be measured through testing.

In the mid-1990s, my internal understanding of my potential came to a crossroads. The direction I would take would be dependent on how I addressed these pressing questions. Do I face my fears or do I retreat? Should I step up or should I take the familiar way out? When the call came from Yale to invite me to be a panelist at the 1996 Yale Journal of Law and Feminism conference *Challenging Boundaries*, with the esteemed law professors Twilla Perry, Ruth-Arlene Howe and Elizabeth Bartholet (each of whom had written extensively on transracial/international adoption), I was scared to death.

In some ways, on the surface, it might have looked like I was well-positioned to speak. I was a social worker who was also a Black transracial adoptee. I had been recruited in 1992 by the world-renowned adoption expert and pioneer, Dr. Joyce Maguire Pavao, to join her pre/post adoption consulting team. But how could I dare to take part in this law panel? I wasn't published, and I didn't have the command of the English language one would need. The last place on earth that I thought I should be was in a debate with a group of law professors who were dead serious about the positions they held on transracial and international adoption.

However, something made me pause; something made me clamp those fears back and begin to think. To think. If I were to accept this invitation what would I want to speak on? What would I want to contribute? What do I have to offer? What is it that might be meaningful to the discussion that could be included in the debate? And I began to think of my experience of being raised in a white environment, within a white Jewish family who had three biological children prior to being one of the first in Massachusetts to begin adopting Black children in the early 1960s. This then led me to feel, both my gratitude for being blessed with having such amazing friends and family, and feelings of disconnectedness and profound sadness resulting from the experience of being racially different over my lifetime.

So there it was. I had identified the only area within the topic of transracial adoption that I wanted to speak on: that of the race experience.

And while I was tossing the idea around, and fearing that I just couldn't get it together to present this experience in a way that it deserved, the internalized presence of my mother became audible. I could hear her say, "Susan, you speak beautifully. Just write the way you speak. Don't worry about what people think or how others write, just write the way you speak. You speak beautifully." And as her internalized voice silenced the insecurities within me, and with the new-found love and inherited gifts that I had been given from my birth mother, I began to creatively write a series of adoption narratives, created slowly by simple sentences, driven by rich feelings and emotions, closely overseen by my clinical insights. The narratives that I created through this process have been used as teaching tools at conferences, events and trainings that I never imagined possible.

This book puts my narratives in one place, including additional text that is not part of the presentations. By converting them to a written form, I hope to make the material accessible to a wide audience of readers. The narratives have stood the test of time in the transracial adoption and adoption community. They are experiential, but are also teaching tools that have helped adoption triad members and professionals of all disciplines make sense of some of the most complicated and challenging issues that transracial adoptees and former foster children face. And, because transracial adoption is so inherently linked to racial identity, they provide an intensely individual perspective on race, culture and identity that I don't believe has been available in other texts.

Massachusetts, October 2012

Acknowledgements

I would like to thank everyone who has ever given me the opportunity to share my narratives at their events, conferences, classrooms or workshops since the mid-1990s. I will forever be appreciative of your warmth, openness, sensitivity and the respect you gave to the subject matter presented.

Next, I would like to thank Dr. Joyce Maguire Pavao for believing in me before I believed in myself, for granting me the opportunity to be part of an amazing professional team of adoption triad members, and for honoring my works so much that you invited them to be heard again and again over the decades in every possible venue.

I would also like to thank Pamela Ogletree and Dr. Kermit Crawford for your ongoing support, and for allowing me the opportunity to continue to develop as a professional and as a human being.

And finally, I would like to thank my husband, Joseph H. O'Connor and my friend, Raymond Pillidge. Without the two of you, this book would never have been possible.

Come Celebrate My First Birthday[1]

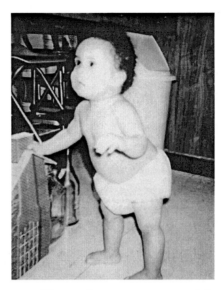

The author at one year old.
The only surviving photo of her in foster care.

In "Come Celebrate My First Birthday," Susan Harris O'Connor discusses the painful and joyous revelations of her search for information regarding the first fourteen months of her life, when her "baby-self" spent this "holding period" in foster care. During this search for her baby-self, Susan discovers that her baby-self was very likely the victim of some of the many types of racial assault depicted in "Can You Imagine?" In telling her story, Susan points out the need for increased attention to adoptive searches that target the holding period, an area of exploration crucial to an adoptee's understanding of herself.

---

[1] "Come Celebrate My First Birthday" was originally published in 1997 in the article: Race, Search and My Baby-Self: Reflections of A Transracial Adoptee. It is reprinted and slightly altered with permission of The Yale Journal of Law and Feminism, Inc. from *The Yale Journal of Law and Feminism*, Vol. 9, Number 1, pp. 5-16.

This paper is written in memory of all the baby-selves who remain missing and unknown. It is also dedicated to my beloved parents, the late Dr. Samuel and Dorothea Rae Harris. For it was their warm bodies, loving arms, and ever-so-gentle voices that eventually embraced and nurtured me in a way that was so desperately needed.

"A tiny bright-faced child, with skin of a deep tone, luminous eyes, and thin dark hair which curls on top of her head. Her small hands are dimpled. She is well formed, though petite."[2]

How beautiful! This is what a psychologist wrote about me when he or she saw me when I was in foster care. What a wonderful feeling it was to find out that someone had actually seen me and had written something so beautiful. That I, at that time, had provoked a smile and a warm feeling in a person. These childhood realities that many of you have been able to take for granted, I have not had the privilege of doing so.

I have often wondered where the numbness comes from. Why, when I look at parents playing with their babies—as if

---

[2] All excerpts in this narrative are taken from notes I found in the file containing information about my stay in foster care during my first fourteen months of life.

everything else in their world is secondary—I am happy for them, though at the same time I feel numb inside. I now know that the numbness has a lot to do with my not having any memories or voices from that period of my life, the time spent in holding.[3] Well, it is time to heal and give voice and memory to my first year of life.

Notes made by a nurse who visited me at the hospital and foster home:

4/11/63: *"This is a normal newborn, active and alert."* *Her skin is white and clear. Okay for foster home placement. At time of discharge, the baby weighed 5 [pounds]-14 [ounces]. Her formula was evaporated milk 8 oz., boiled water 16 oz., 2 1/2 tbsp. Karo syrup. There is a probability that the father of this infant has a negro Indian racial background."*

4/13/63: *"The baby is nursing well. She takes 2 - 2 1/2 oz. at a feeding. There is no vomiting and the stools are normal."*

-----

[3] I define the "holding period" as the time after a child is surrendered for adoption until the child enters the adoptive home. It is common for a child in the United States to spend this holding period in the care of the state.

4/23/63: *"The baby weighs 6 [pounds] - 4 [ounces]. She takes 3 oz. of formula every four hours. There is no spitting or vomiting. She has black hair. Her skin appears to be white."*

4/30/63: *"Today the baby's general skin tone looks somewhat dusky."*

5/8/63: *"Baby weighs 7 [pounds]- 2 [ounces] and is 20 inches long."* [I had to have been so cute.] *"Her skin coloring has become definitely dusk[y]. [T]he palms of her hands are pink. She follows with her eyes, but does not smile yet in response to attention."*

6/20/63: *"Today the baby really smiles in response to attention."*

8/21/63: *"The foster family has been away on vacation. The baby weighs 12 lbs. She is negroid in appearance, particularly the skin tone, which is quite dark. Her hair is sparse, black and tends to curl. Her eyes are brown. The nares are broad, but the mouth is small. Her social responses are definitely slow. She does not smile spontaneously, even to foster mother."*

Interesting. Was it coincidental that the day the nurse found me negroid in appearance was the same day I was found to be "definitely" slow in social responsiveness? Why the ongoing attention placed on the question of my race?[4] It was one thing for the nurse to state that I am African American, or at that time negroid. The way in which this nurse focused on my racial appearance, however, would make me believe that I was defective. Is a white child observed like this? With a focus on the child's nares, hair, and mouth? What did these findings mean to the nurse?[5] Didn't she understand that my features and skin coloring were nothing out of the ordinary? I was just a Jewish multiracial baby in a foreign place—being viewed by a person who could not relate.

Remember, this is the only information that I, an adoptee, will ever have about my first year of life. The thought that someone might have objectified me at that age was very painful for me to learn. Being a transracial adoptee who was raised in a

---

[4] Why was the nurse so interested in the "probability" of my birth father's racial background? There was no "probability" that he was of African and Native American descent; if she had looked in my records file, she would have discovered he was "definitely" a person of color.

[5] Would my being negroid bring in less or no money for the agency? Would this delay my adoption process or categorize me as an "unadoptable or undesirable" baby to a white Jewish adoption agency?

white environment, this type of objectification has been a familiar theme in my life. But to again encounter the racism of others in my search for my lost roots, to realize that I as an innocent, vulnerable baby was the victim of racism adds another complicated and deep layer of sadness and pain to my search. This is not to say that the nurse was racist on a conscious level; she could have made unconscious racist associations. But the harm to me today and to my baby-self cannot be undone.

"A tiny, dark complexioned child, with luminous eyes, and thin, curly, dark hair. Her skin is of a deep tone, her features small, in keeping with her build. She is well-formed, with dimpled hands."

I think I will hold on to this, the psychologist's description of me—it is very comforting.

On 9/13/63, when I was five months old, the psychologist administered Gesell Normative testing. S/he determined that *"her quick social responsiveness is appealing."*

Soon afterward, the nurse wrote:

10/4/63: *"The baby weighs 13 lbs. She has spurted ahead in her development in the last 6-8 weeks and was most sociable and responsive. She rolls to navigate, and gets to a creeping position and rocks. She bears full weight when held upright. She eats well, and is on a full diet, 3 meals a day."*

Interesting. Was it coincidental that the nurse suddenly observed that I had spurted ahead developmentally after the psychologist had found my social responsiveness appealing? Or was the nurse's initial impression of me subjective and possibly racist, so that she quickly changed her opinion of me once the report came back? Who knows? We will never know. I can tell you that the tears I shed while absorbing this foster care information about myself contained both joy and sadness. Joy for discovering the positive qualities I possessed at that age, and sadness thinking about how vulnerable my baby-self had been in foster care.

Do any of you actually have any idea of how powerful an impact search and finding can have on the adoptee?[6] That

---

[6] To learn more about the experiences of adoptees who search for their birth families, see Phyllis R. Silverman, et al., Reunions between adoptees and birth parents: The adoptees' experience. *Social Work*, July 1991, 329-35.

immediately following my first conversation with my birth mother,[7] it dawned on me that I had been walking on my knees my entire life, and that I no longer had to do so because I had just been given my feet. That for me finding both my birth families helped me make sense of so many things. For example, I now know who I resemble in looks, personality, and talent. I also know what makes me unique. Meeting my birth mother gave voice to the fact that I really came out of a real woman's body, not an imaginary one. That pregnancy can be a beautiful and natural experience. That I had a real beginning to life similar to yours. That my life did not begin when I was adopted; that in fact, my life began when my birth mother gave birth to me.

One might think that because I found my birth families years ago, my days of searching were over. But after years of knowing my birth families and being able to integrate the similarities and differences into my life, it became apparent to me that there was still something missing. And it became much more obvious to me while I watched parents playing with their babies

---

[7] I choose to call my mother who carried me for nine months prior to me being placed for adoption, my birth mother. She and I have used this term over the course of our relationship since finding each other some twenty-two years ago. However, another term that is more recently being used is 'first' mother or 'first' father. There are a growing number of people who would prefer to use this term.

that the numb feeling I felt came from not knowing anything about that particular time in my life. That time period was non-existent to me, to my birth families, and to my adoptive family. It was a lengthy period of my life that had never been talked about. It had never been made real to me because no one I knew had ever been with my baby-self during those first fourteen months. This lack of information, stimulation, and discussion regarding my baby-self, I now know, through the years had an injurious emotional effect on me.

The interplay between parents and babies really made me think. Who held me at that age?! Was I held? Did someone find my baby-self absolutely irresistible? Who talked baby talk to me? Did someone cheer for my baby-self when she made various movements or when her first tooth erupted?! Did someone help her regain composure after she was relinquished at birth? So many questions unanswered. So many feelings dead and asleep.

The importance of pictures, lifebooks, and other works that so many professionals and parents have created to chronicle children's time in foster care, and which are now used to soften the difficult journey for foster children and adoptees, cannot be overstated. These aids attempt to create an ongoing narrative for children to forever have as they travel through placements, preventing them from having more gaps and unknowns in their lives than need be.

Think about how common a phenomenon it is that a parent of a newborn pulls out her baby pictures to proudly show others how the adorable baby resembles her mother or father or some other relative. When a child is raised by her biological family, the parent(s) are able to observe their child's development and pass on their observations of the child's similarities and differences as compared to themselves and other family members, creating a life-long conversation between parent and child. By the time the child becomes an adult, she may take for granted all the knowledge about family heredity when she herself bears a child. All this, which most people take for granted, adoptees cannot. This is not to say that all adoptees have an interest in discovering information about the holding period, or that they are the only individuals who do not have this information. But it is important to recognize that for adoptees who do conduct this type of search, the cognitive-emotional process of searching is complex and can be painful.

The search can be especially difficult for the adoptee if family members and counseling professionals minimize the process.[8] They may dismiss the adoptee's search for information about the holding period, believing that finding this information is not that important. But these people, who were likely raised within their biological families, overlook the fact that they have had access to this type of information throughout the years. They have baby pictures. They have been able to ask family members about their early childhood.

"In prone she mounted on hands, tilting her head and smiling. From this position she is reported to turn over. She came to sit, from supine, her face eager, and she sat alone briefly. She also bore her full weight actively. Impressive was her quick interest in the cubes, her eyes traveling to the single one, and her attention sustained as she subsequently grasped, dropped, and

---

[8] This search process can also be difficult for the birth parents and adoptive family. For birth parents, particularly birth mothers, this search by the adoptee for foster care data can immediately place them once again in a place of guilt, shame, and anger. They might have thought that they were through learning what had happened to their child, never thinking that the adoptee would actually seek out additional foster placement information. For birth mothers of color and white birth mothers impregnated by men of color, who were made to believe that their child would be immediately adopted, learning detailed information of a lengthy foster care stay that is tainted with racism can be additionally painful. For the adoptive family, there may be a sense of –here we go again. Family members may feel guilt and fear that they have not met their child's needs because once again, the child is searching for more. Sadness and pain regarding infertility issues of the adoptive parents may also resurface. Of course, one cannot generalize how families are going to handle this part of the search. It can be a very positive and non-threatening experience.

secured another. Her right hand was most active, but when she finally secured one left, she held it longer, and retained a second.'' [Of course, I am left-handed.] *"Her only recurrent interest in the bell, its ringing and cup, seemed to stem from fatigue, her effort spent on the cubes.''*

How can I not overflow with teary delight as I think about how my baby-self mounted on her hands, tilted her head, and smiled? I now have somewhat of a visual picture of how I moved and how absolutely irresistible I must have been as a baby.

So it is with these foster care notes that I have been able to piece together part of my life history, and put together various images of my baby-self that I will forever have. And it is these images that will over time help dissolve the numbness.

This is the last entry in the notes made by the nurse prior to my first birthday:

3/24/64: *"Baby is really adorable, definitely negroid in appearance. The nares are somewhat broad, her mouth* *comparatively small. Her first tooth erupted two weeks ago, and three more since that time."*

I can't help but to glow! We all know how adorable babies are when they are showing their first teeth. Can't you just see my baby-self right now? With two tiny teeth on the top of her mouth and two tiny teeth on the bottom. Yes! It is time to regress, to integrate, to heal, and to celebrate.

Just as finding my birth mother gave me my FEET, obtaining foster care information about my holding period has given me my ANKLES.

When I contacted my former foster mother, a white Christian woman who had over a twenty-year period parented only Jewish babies, I asked her if she remembered me? She said, "no" without emotion. I immediately knew that I could not get emotional because it appeared as if she had dealt with foster care in a rather robotic way. When I asked her if she could have been the one who named me, she replied, "No, I wouldn't have given you that name." When I asked if she had had a difficult time when children left her home, she said, "It was a matter of fact. I knew that none of you would be staying because you were Jewish so there was no reason to become attached." I thought to myself, how could a person not become attached to newborn children, especially one who had been there for fourteen months? It was at this time that I realized there was a great possibility that I had never had a first birthday party. That my first birthday might have just come and gone without any type of acknowledgment or celebration.

My tiny bright-faced child, with skin of a deep tone, luminous eyes, and thin dark hair which curls on top of your head. You, with your four teeth, and an adorable Jewish/Black/Indian nose, no longer have to deal with the bittersweet alone. Tossing and turning, without anyone watching over you who truly loves you.

I know that those first fourteen months were hard and that not all of your needs were met. You see, I know you quite well, and know that at the time of adoption, you were delayed and starved for attention.

The fact that you had a nurse and caretaker who did not love and adore you was by no means a reflection of you. You see, you were and still are so very lovable and worthy of all that is good. HAPPY BIRTHDAY! Precious One! Any parent would have been fortunate to have had you.

The author being held by her sister Barbara, at 15 months old.

"Come Celebrate My First Birthday" was presented at:

2012. Course presenter with child welfare expert Kim Stevens, *Harris Autobiographical Narratives*, Rhode Island College School of Social Work Continuing Education.

2011. Featured narrative trilogy, Boston University Medical Campus/Center for Multicultural Training in Psychology.

2008. Featured performance, Center for Family Connections 7th Annual *Courage and Curiosity Celebration*, MA.

2007. Featured performance, (PACT Camp) Pact Adoption Alliance summer retreat, California.

2006. Keynote performance, St. John's College Adoption Conference, New York.

2006. Featured speaker, Wayside Youth and Families, Massachusetts.

2003. Keynote address, Connecticut Department of Children and Families.

2003. Keynote address, New Hampshire Department of Children, Youth and Families.

2003. Presentation, After Adoption and Center for Family Connection, *First International Adoption Practice Conference* in Dublin, Ireland.

2002. Featured speaker, Justice Resource Institute/Southeast Commonworks training series, Massachusetts.

2002. Presentation, Center for Family Connections, Massachusetts.

2002. Keynote address, Department of Children, Youth and Family/Rhode Island conference, *Building Partnership through Family Centered Practice*.

2002. Featured speaker, event hosted by A Red Thread, Massachusetts.

2001. Featured speaker, Massachusetts Society for the Protection of Cruelty to Children, Cape Cod.

2001. Featured speaker, Smith College School of Social Work, Massachusetts.

2001. Keynote performance, The Bridge of Central Massachusetts.

2001. Keynote address, Massachusetts Department of Youth Services, annual conference for educators.

2001. Keynote address, Massachusetts Department of Mental Health annual conference.

2000. Event to feature narratives, Casey Family Services, Portland, Maine.

2000. Featured presentation, Catholic Charities conference, Merrimack Valley Regional Office, Massachusetts.

2000. Event to feature a narrative trilogy, Children's Aid and Family Services/Adoption Crossroads-Western Region, Massachusetts.

1999. Featured presentation, University of New Hampshire.

1999. Classroom presentation, University of Maine.

1999. Featured presentation, CASA (Court Appointed Special Advocate), Rhode Island.

1999. Plenary speaker, *Child Protection: Meeting The Challenges* seminar, The Judicial Branch and the Office of the Child Advocate of the State of Connecticut.

1999. Classroom presentation, Boston College School of Social Work, Massachusetts.

1999. Featured narrative trilogy, Casey Family Services, Warwick, Rhode Island.

1999. Featured narrative trilogy, The Adoption Connection annual conference, Massachusetts.

1999. Featured narrative trilogy, Massachusetts General Hospital/The Archway Interdisciplinary Adoption Study Group, led by Dr. Steven Nickman and Dr. Linda Forsythe.

1999. Keynote performance, narrative trilogy, National Adoption Congress, McLean, Virginia.

1999. Featured narrative trilogy, *Second Annual Statewide Conference for Educators*, Massachusetts.

1999. Featured presentation, Communities For People, Inc., Massachusetts.

1999. Presentation, Black Administrators in Child Welfare, Annual Symposium, Washington, D.C.

1999. Lecturer, Cambridge Series Conference: *Clinical Issues in Adoption* facilitated by Dr. Joyce Maguire Pavao, Massachusetts.

1998. Featured narrative trilogy, Governor's Commission on Child Placement in Foster and Adoptive Care for the State of Rhode Island.

1998. Presentation, The Adoption Connection conference, Massachusetts.

1998. Keynote address, *Foster Parent Appreciation Day*, Massachusetts Department of Social Services, Fitchburg, Massachusetts.

1997. Presentation, American Adoption Congress, New York, New York.

1997. Classroom presentation, Boston College School of Social Work, Massachusetts.

1997. Keynote address, Worcester Public Schools, personnel development for clinical faculty, Worcester, Massachusetts.

A Relationship With A Birth Father:
Reflections of a Transracial Adoptee

Originally written and performed in 1998.

In this article, Susan Harris O'Connor presents her personal story to enlighten and educate adoption, foster care professionals and adoptive, birth, or foster families on the impact an unknown birth parent can have on a person's psyche. Susan is tri-racial and was adopted in 1964 by a white couple. She was raised in a predominately white environment and her adoptive parents informed her at an early age that her birth mother was white and her birth father was of African and Native American descent. Her adoption was a closed adoption and very little birth history had been given to the Harris family.

This paper is a tribute to the man who sired me, Mr. Barry W. It salutes the memories and fantasies that keep loved ones alive.

My birth father! Yes, it is true that I have mourned this unknown entity. This man with an unknown identity. I'll never know why I have such strong feelings for a person I have never met, but I do. It has been a very challenging journey trying to make sense of how this particular loss has manifested itself within me. How it has woven itself into my psyche.

28

The impact of this loss, I now realize, embodies a silent side of me – that of a very private and secretive relationship.[9] A particularly bizarre situation that I have had to experience alone. I had no idea how to make sense of and/or articulate the rippling effects of this injury. Fortunately, I am now able to share my story of how this loss propelled me into a one-sided relationship with my birth father consisting of daydreams and magical thinking.

In 1990, I was told that he had stood 6' 2" and had had a
sculptured body like a Greek God!
That when he walked, people were startled
by his magnificent dark black body.
That he had been a sensitive man who would have
kept me and married her way back in 1963.
That while she thought of him and looked at me she
could see that we had at least one thing
in common:
our good looking feet!

[9] "Once an adoptee is made aware of adoptive status, mental construction of the absent progenitors becomes necessary, and the internal dialogue between an adoptee and his or her inner representation or construction of the birth parents is as much a relationship as the connection between a bereaved individual and the dead person." (Nickman, 1996, p. 257) in Klass, D., Silverman, P.R. and Nickman, S. (Eds). Continuing bonds: *New Understandings of grief.* Taylor and Francis: Washington, DC.

That last comment was the remark that I had been waiting for, the one that would re-root me. The one that validated our shared biology, the one statement that sent me into a fantasy of me and my birth father sitting on the beach, hanging out so innocently, admiring our good looking feet.

After I had returned from this sweet fantasy of being connected to my birth father through our feet, I wanted more! More of me, more of him, because having more of him would give me more of me. I then asked my birth mother, "Is that it?! Can't you see more of him in me?" She gently replied, "No, Susan, not really," and went immediately to locate the pictures of him she had saved for me. And while she looked for the pictures, I thought of my feet, and hurriedly returned to the hot sunny beach because my birth father and I were busy, busy at the beach, being mesmerized by our good looking feet. (I must say that my positive foot image has grown even stronger since that day!)

When my birth mother returned with two pictures of my birth father at approximately 27 years of age, I was immediately confused. Looking at the pictures of this man who was at the age that I was at the time was alarming. I was relieved that his look did not move me sexually. That would be the last type of fantasy I would want to explore.[10] Another issue was that I couldn't see a physical resemblance. His skin coloring and facial features were so different from mine. Because I grew up believing that he would naturally look like me, I now knew I would have to mourn the loss of this belief because it wasn't based in reality.

The inability to see a resemblance between me and my birth father, and the newness of my relationship with my White birth mother put an immediate halt to my desire to physically search for him. But it did not stop me from having my own type of relationship with him, which began like this:

How could you do this to me?! How could you make it so that I can't see me?! You are one of two people in the world who are supposed to look like me. Don't you remember that you helped to create me; that you are the only connection that I have

---

[10] For more information about this topic please refer to Childs R. (1998). *Genetic sexual attraction: Healing and danger in the reunions of adoptees and their birth families.* Unpublished doctoral dissertation, Massachusetts School of Professional Psychology.
Adoptees who feel vulnerable being with a particular birth relative(s) might benefit from obtaining support from a clinician who is knowledgeable and sensitive to genetic sexual attraction issues. It might also help for the adoptee to avoid being alone with the person(s) with whom sh/e feels vulnerable until such feelings subside. Although the prevalence of this phenomenon is unknown, adoptees, professionals and birth/adoptive/foster family members should take note of this issue.

to my Black identity? And as the tears flowed from me, he gently hugged me and allowed me to grieve the loss of him, the loss of a part of me, and the shattering of a lifetime of fantasies.

I believe I moved in and out of this daydream for about two years, frequently looking at his pictures and crying myself to sleep. And then one day it dawned on me after I had moved on in grieving that we must have had other things in common. As I stared at his pictures, and thought of him and me, I then realized that, of course, we both had black skin coloring. So with the two of us in my thoughts, constructed unconsciously by my desperate need to fill this missing part, we immediately took off to familiarize ourselves with our shared oppressed skin. There was no way that I could remain saddened by this sensitive man. I was just extremely happy to be with him and to hear him speak about anything. If only my magical thoughts would have the power to bring him to life![11,12]

---

[11] Fantasies that stem from a significant loss, such as the loss of a birth parent, can be quite powerful. Professionals and parents can reach out by simply initiating a non-intrusive, non-voyeuristic, non-judgmental, age-appropriate conversation periodically that allows the adoptee if (s)he chooses to discuss birth parent thoughts and fantasies. These conversations may help to reduce the isolation and shame the fantasies can sometimes generate. Furthermore, sensitivity to fantasies can serve as support to the adoptee in the grieving process, and can also serve as support while the individual is involved in a search for her birth parent. Individuals can become emotionally vulnerable when a fantasy they have believed in is found to be untrue.

32

The desire to meet my birth father became all-encompassing once the intensity of my relationship with my birth mother leveled off.[13] It was as if my merging and then separating from my birth mother, and sorting through our relationship and my fantasies, freed me to focus solely on my birth father. Would he be alive and doing well? Or would he be struggling with societal ills? All I hoped was that he hadn't been found dead—hanging—like all too many innocent Black men!

A detective located my birth father's family rather quickly once I initiated the search. I was deeply anguished when a

---

In addition, professionals and parents (who may possess important birth parent information) can help the adoptee decipher what is real in the daydreams. Legal professionals and adoption social workers assist in determining whether adoptive parent(s) receive an accurate and detailed child and birth family history. If the information is inaccurate, the adoptee faces the risk of internalizing false information and images that will later be contradicted when the truth is learned.

[12] Fantasies can also be quite intense for a birth parent who has spent years wondering about what ever happened to his or her child. An adoptive parent can also have powerful fantasies about the biological child she/he had wished to have. Even in my family situation where my parents actually raised six children, three biological and three adopted, my mother silently grieved and fantasized about her first baby, a baby boy, who had arrived as a still born.

[13] This period of being completely absorbed with finding a birth parent is considered by Dr. Joyce Maguire Pavao (author of *Normative Crisis in Adoption*) a normative crisis. It is a time where it is not uncommon to find the adoptee/foster youth, adult having difficulty focusing on significant tasks and/or people. A time when they are desperately awaiting to hear back from people who are assisting them in their search. For some, it might mean arranging a sudden trip to their birth place, and/or joining a support group with other people who are at various stages of the search. Each search, and the way in which the individual conducts and processes the search, varies greatly. It is important to note that not all adoptees search for both birth parents. Nor does every adoptee have an interest in or desire to search for either birth parent. However, an adoptee who doesn't have a current interest to search may later change her or his thoughts and initiate a search at any point in time.

relative informed me that Barry hadn't been heard from in over twenty-five years. When the detective told me that Barry was dead, and that secrecy surrounded his death, the news sent me into a secretive place where my thoughts and fantasies became even more developed and intense.

How could he do this to me?! How could he make it so that I can't see me?! He was one of two people in the world who was supposed to be looking for me! Had he forgotten that he was supposed to be alive and waiting for me? That he was supposed to help me in my internal journey to feel more complete? As my heart overflowed with sadness, my deceased adoptive parents suddenly appeared. They gently hugged me and allowed me to grieve the death of him, the death of a part of me that harbored such beautiful yet unrealistic fantasies. (I now understand that fantasies could actually comfort me while at the same time creating additional complexities.)

Approximately two years passed before I felt emotionally ready to call my paternal birth family again. And there I was, within one week, visiting a southern state for the first time, meeting all of my Black living relatives. Relatives and friends of his said to me, "Your father could have accomplished anything." And of course, you know I believed them!

On my return home from the South, a part of me felt complete, and a part of me felt empty. I found it emotionally difficult to grieve Barry while I was also internalizing the sadness, beauty and realness of my blackness. As time passed, I began to feel comfortable with all that I had experienced. And one evening, while I sat at home thinking about how at peace I was feeling, I realized that I had suddenly turned into a beautiful dancer, a *ballerina*. Now I didn't mind being a ballerina for a couple of hours, but what was it about this daydream that made me return to it repeatedly? What made dancing in front of this magical audience so very comforting? Was there someone of importance who I hoped would be there watching? Then it struck me that this was a birth father fantasy; that my psyche was subtly telling me that it was time to do more grieving. It was only a matter of seconds before he vividly appeared, and I found myself toe-dancing while holding his beautiful black hands. My dear birth father. May he and my adoptive mother and father all rest together in peace.

Shortly after this series of daydreams, I realized why my lifetime of birth father daydreams were so painfully striking. It was not their frequency or the intensity in which they arrived. Nor was it necessarily the content or the feelings that they provoked. What made them so striking was that they actually marked the full extent of my physical and emotional relationship with him; that my relationship with him, has always been and will forever be based in a fantasy! Another layer of loss for me to grieve.

"Barry, do you mind if I hold your resting body while I pay tribute to you? I know for a fact that you didn't have an easy life. That you came from a broken family, grew up in abject poverty and then, later, got lost while drifting. These realities don't make me think less of you. It is still extremely easy for me to care about you because you helped to create me! What better gift could you have given to me, my friends and my families?

If I tell you a secret will you promise me that you will keep it from people who would only view me as being narcissistic?

Now —when I look at your pictures—I see me—and see that like you—I really am quite a beauty." [14]

The author.

---

[14] Stanford Professor Larry Friedlander, a friend of my birth mother who remembers meeting my birth father in Harvard Square back in 1962, wrote the following excerpt for me:

"Watching Barry walk, or waltz, down the street was a trip. He had the most extraordinary physical presence, a kind of energy that radiated from him and that made people just stop and stare. It was partly due to his actual build—massive shoulders, tiny waist, jaunty butt; partly due to a kind of grace and dance-like quality in his movements; partly due to his big smile and his stare, making easy contact with all he passed; but finally it was something in his spirit, a kind of joy in being alive and in being present on the earth that just flowed from him."

"A Relationship With A Birth Father: Reflections of A Transracial Adoptee" was presented at:

2012. Course presenter with child welfare expert, Kim Stevens, *Harris Autobiographical Narratives*, Rhode Island College School of Social Work continuing education.

2002. Workshop presentation, Child Welfare League of America annual conference, Florida.

2000. Event to feature a narrative trilogy, Children's Aid and Family Services/Adoption Crossroads-Western Region, Massachusetts.

1999. Featured presentation, CASA (Court Appointed Special Advocate), Rhode Island.

1999. Plenary speaker, seminar titled *Child Protection: Meeting The Challenges*, The Judicial Branch and the Office of the Child Advocate of the State of Connecticut.

1999. Featured classroom presentation, Boston College School of Social Work, Massachusetts.

1999. Featured narrative trilogy, Casey Family Services, Warwick, Rhode Island.

1999. Featured narrative trilogy, The Adoption Connection's annual conference, Massachusetts.

1999. Featured narrative trilogy, Massachusetts General Hospital/The Archway Interdisciplinary Adoption Study Group, led by Dr. Steven Nickman and Dr. Linda Forsythe.

1999. Keynote address, narrative trilogy, National Adoption Congress, McLean, Virginia.

1999. Featured narrative trilogy, Second Annual Statewide Conference for Educators, Massachusetts.

1999. Presentation, Black Administrators in Child Welfare Annual Symposium, Washington, D.C.

1999. Presented (per request/unplanned) Cambridge Series Conference, *Clinical Issues in Adoption*, facilitated by Dr. Joyce Maguire Pavao.

1998. Featured narrative trilogy, Governor's Commission on Child Placement in Foster and Adoptive Care for the State of Rhode Island.

1998. Presentation, The Adoption Connection conference, Massachusetts.

1998. Featured presentation, Center for Family Connections, *Summer Intensive Course in Adoption and Blended Family Studies*, Provincetown, Massachusetts.

Can You Imagine?[15]

The author as a child.

Susan Harris O'Connor gives voice to the realities of her experiences as a transracial adoptee and the experiences of other persons of color adopted into white families. "Can You Imagine?" is a narrative of stories pieced together and drawn from the stories of transracial adoptees whom Susan has met, counseled, and known. It unmasks the unique complexities of race and racism, so often ignored, in the lives of transracial adoptees, and challenges adoptive families and adoption professionals to honestly confront the role of race in the adoption process.

---

[15] "Can You Imagine?" was first published in the article: Race, Search and My Baby-Self: Reflections of a Transracial Adoptee. The narrative was created for and presented at the 1996 Yale conference, *Challenging Boundaries*. It is reprinted and slightly altered with permission of The Yale Journal of Law and Feminism, Inc. from *The Yale Journal of Law and Feminism*, (1997).Vol. 9, Number 1, pp. 5-16.

Have you ever spent time imagining

what it would have been like

to have been raised among individuals who were racially different

from you?

What it would have been like

to have gone FOR YEARS never having

spoken to a person who was of the same race as you?

What it would have been like

throughout the course of a typical day

never to encounter a person

who looked like you?

What it would have been like

to have EVen your own *PARents* be

of a different race from you?

Can you imagine?

Let's think about this even though it might be hard to conceptualize. I am not talking about spending time abroad to experience different cultures or foods, knowing all the time that regardless of how you are treated, you will be able to return home and blend in with your family, friends, and peers. Nor am I talking about hanging out with friends of a different race, class, or culture and feeling different and sometimes uncomfortable for obvious and/or sometimes not-obvious reasons, yet knowing all the while that you can leave, and find a person

who will

understand you,

mirror you,

and once again, remind you,

that you are okay being the way you are. I am not talking about the choices you have made to become a more cultivated person. I am not talking about choices. And I am definitely not talking about a bad hair day.

I am talking about growing up in a town where there might be one, two, three or four persons—if you're lucky—who look like you, but are not necessarily your age or even people with whom you are likely to come into contact. This is the situation for many transracial/transcultural adoptees who come from closed adoptions and who are raised in predominately white communities. The African American transracial adoptee has facial features and/or skin coloring which have been historically exploited and oppressed (as do other racial/ethnic groups).

The author with her sister, Barbara.

Can you imagine an adorable little African American girl in the first grade who comes home daily crying to mommy that the white children were laughing at her funny hair? And one day she arrives home to report that her nickname is nigger, not knowing that it is a racist remark. Can you imagine the pain the child's parents struggle with after learning that their sweet, innocent child is already being violated at the age of six?

OR how about a little African American boy who is constantly picked on and called nigger by his peers at school. In addition, he has a teacher who ignores him and will not teach him. All the while his parents who are white have no idea what is happening. Why would they? It is not their experience. How could they think that people would do such things to their child?

OR how about the black child who is singled out by his teacher because he is black and must know about black history. Only this causes the child great discomfort because he does not even know another black person, never mind black history.

Can you imagine being the only person of color in your school and community? Which would set you up to be the black token and likely target for many racist assaults from both peers and adults. Assaults that are overt or covert, intentional or unintentional, conscious or unconscious, direct or indirect. Assaults that many times both child and parent had no idea occurred, not until later on in life. Is this a healthy environment for the transracial adoptive family? Is this the way to integrate a white community?

What happens to the black male when he enters the adolescent years? This of course varies from male to male. How will he be viewed by various white people as he begins to look like a black man? Think of the confusion the adoptee might have if he is surrounded by white people who view him as a token, tell him that he isn't really black, and proceed to talk negatively about those other blacks. Or what must it be like to hear your white peers chat about getting a "black" one in the sack? How does the black male feel if he is viewed as a token one day, and then the next is falsely accused (like so many black males) of being a liar and/or a thief? Will he encounter fearful, racist white men who become angry and retaliate when he gets a position that they feel their white sons should have had? Will any of the white adults become concerned that the black male might date or rape their "superior or angelic" white daughters? Can you imagine the pain, rage, and confusion a black transracial adoptee has if and when he figures out that the environment he was raised in did not and does not value him or what he represents—black men?

What happens to the black female when dating begins? How does the black female feel about herself if all of her friends who are white begin to date and she is left dateless? How does she approach this subject with her white peers and white parents? Will anyone be sensitive to her? Or will people use the color-blind approach? Who knows? It really is the luck of the draw. Can you imagine having some of your friends say to you, "Maybe the boys don't ask you out because you're not friendly enough?" Could this be the case throughout all twelve years of schooling? I should say not! The black female, however, could easily believe her friends and think there is something wrong with her.

Will the black female lose some friends if she says she doesn't get dates because she is not liked because she is black? Who knows? This can play out in numerous ways. What happens if the black female gets angry with her friends and family for not understanding her situation? Will they think she's crazy because Bobby, the boy she likes, would never be prejudiced? Will they think she is just race obsessed, that she always blames these things on race? Will some of her friends feel justified to think of her as or call her a black bitch? Can you imagine going through twelve years of schooling supposedly like all of your white girlfriends, but never having a white boyfriend, or if you are gay, a white girlfriend? Or can you imagine being sexually exploited by so many boys, while all that you wanted was what your friends had—a boyfriend? Can you imagine none of your friends, parents, or even your white therapist (if you have one) ever bringing up the topic of race while things like this are happening to you? On an intellectual level, it would make sense because race does not play a significant part in their lives. But I strongly believe it does for many transracial adoptees whether they or their parents know it.

How does a white adoptive father and his adult black daughter make sense of a situation when they are together and someone believes her to be a prostitute? How does the daughter feel about her sense of worth if this is just one of many times that she has been told and made to feel worthless just because she wears a coat of color and has features that are African?

Can you imagine going through life being the target of discrimination when you have never seen or met a black person who is biologically related to you? How does one make sense of this? How can a person be called a nigger or a black bitch when she has been surrounded and only loved by white people? Race must be a social construct. So is this a color-blind society?

Imagine at some point in your life being exposed to your same race and not being accepted because you are acting too "white." Is this an act? Why would anyone think that a child of any color raised by white parents in a white community would be anything other than a white person who has been spray painted one of the various shades of color? How do you think it feels when you begin to see that you have been too "socialized white" to feel "black," and too dark-skinned to ever be accepted as white?

What happens if the transracial adoptee seeks out therapy from within the white community? What is the likelihood that there will be a therapist who is knowledgeable and fluent in race-related issues especially if there are no people of color, particularly African Americans, who work within the agency? Can you imagine having a therapist of any color who is ignorant and uncomfortable talking about race and adoption-related issues, but at the same time is eager to meet with you, to learn from you about the transracial adoptee experience? Imagine paying money to a therapist who occasionally causes you to become emotionally distraught (just like so many others have done) because he or she is at times unable to mask his or her racist point(s) of view. This

can be an extremely difficult, exploitive, humiliating, and psychologically damaging journey.

Let's think about this for a moment. How long do you think it takes to make a child of color shut down and become sealed over especially when all of the child's support systems consist of white people who visibly mirror the people who have caused him or her harm and discomfort? Or how many racist remarks, attitudes, and/or cues do you think it takes to ruin a child's positive sense of self? One, two, three, four, five racist remarks over the course of a ten-year period? Three racist remarks in the fourth grade? Or how about one extremely powerful racist sexual remark right at the time of puberty? You know what kinds of remarks I'm talking about. The type of remarks that speak to the size of the black man's penis or the ones that sexualize and dehumanize the black woman. I know I cannot answer these questions for you. Can you?

By now I'm sure that most of you think I am completely opposed to transracial adoption. Guess what? You are quite wrong. I loved my parents, and I know that they loved me. I would not have traded them in for anyone, although I would have traded the all-white environment for an integrated one. And I know plenty of transracial adoptees who feel the same.

Just because I educate people on the realities of racism that play out in this type of a situation—the realities I have learned through readings, clinical practice, friendships, colleagues, and most importantly my own personal story—doesn't mean that I am opposed to transracial adoption. Life isn't just about BLACK or WHITE, RIGHT or WRONG, GREAT or AWFUL, ALL or NOTHING. Life to me is about GREY MATTER, or like being on a continuum. Sometimes it is okay to adopt transracially and other times it is not. Sometimes the environment is great for the transracial adoptive family, and other times it might vary from okay to what I call *toxic*. Some transracial adoptees have done quite well academically and career-wise, however, at the same time shuttling in and out of therapeutic settings. And just because there are transracial adoptees who haven't had major difficulties doesn't mean that there isn't a continuing need to address the underlying and overriding issues that play themselves out in adoption. I believe that people need to be educated on the issues that are present so that they can make informed decisions.

So who is responsible for making sure that the human needs of the transracial adoptee are appropriately met? Who is going to see to it that white adoptive and prospective adoptive parents get educated about such realities so that some of these dehumanizing experiences can be prevented or minimized? I know there are many people who believe education regarding race and adoptee-related issues is not necessary and that love is enough. I strongly disagree. Love is necessary, but how does the black child who will eventually grow up to be a black adult have a chance to love him or herself if he or she is the ongoing target of discrimination? Especially if there is no place for the child and the family to go to regularly to get mirrored, validated, and made to see that it is more than okay to be of a blended family.

It is critical that white parents be aware that the power of racism is so great that it can sabotage all the time, energy, and love they put into raising their child of color. If the parent is not astute and able to guide the child through and around the realities of racism and adoptee related issues, and set up a multiracial/multicultural support system, or live in an integrated community that includes both children and adults of color, the child can be severely damaged emotionally, psychologically, and sometimes physically. The better prepared the parents, siblings, and extended family are, the better chance the child and the family will have.[16]

---

[16] To learn more about the complicated life experiences of transracial adoptees, see Steven L. Nickman, The Adoption Experience. (1985); Ruth G. McRoy & Louis A. Zurcher Jr., Transracial and Interracial Adoptees: The Adolescent Years. (1983); Era Bell Thompson, *The adoption controversy; Blacks who grew up in White homes*. Ebony, June 1974, p. 84. To learn more about the complexities of being a transcultural adoptee, see generally Dick Lehr, *The riddle of Julia Ming Gale*, Boston Globe, Oct 8, 1996, E1; Steve Fainaru, *Imeldo (Gina) struggles for identity*, Boston Globe, July 15, 1996, A6; Dottie Enrico, *How I learned I wasn't Caucasian*, Glamour, Sept. 1995, 106.

52

"Can You Imagine?" was presented at:

1999. Featured narrative trilogy, Casey Family Services, Warwick, Rhode Island.

1999. Featured narrative trilogy, The Adoption Connection annual conference, Massachusetts.

1999. Featured narrative trilogy, Massachusetts General Hospital/The Archway Interdisciplinary Adoption Study Group, led and founded by Dr. Steven Nickman and Dr. Linda Forsythe.

1999. Keynote performance, narrative trilogy, National Adoption Congress, McLean, Virginia.

1999. Featured narrative trilogy, Second Annual Statewide Conference for Educators, Massachusetts.

1998. Featured narrative trilogy, Governor's Commission on Child Placement in Foster and Adoptive Care for the State of Rhode Island.

1997. Presentation, *American Adoption Congress Conference*, New York.

1997. Classroom presentation, University of Maine.

1997. Classroom presentation, Boston College School of Social Work.

1997. Keynote address, Worcester Public Schools, personnel development for clinical faculty, Massachusetts.

1997. Presentation, Massachusetts Department of Social Services Statewide Council for People of Color conference.

1997. Lecturer, Cambridge Series conference, *The Many Phases in Adoption,* facilitated by Dr. Joyce Maguire Pavao, Massachusetts.

1996. Created for and presented at the Yale Journal of Law and Feminism conference, *Challenging Boundaries*. The other panelists were Susan Cox and law professors Elizabeth Bartholet, Ruth-Arlene Howe and Twilla Perry.

The Harris Racial Identity Theory:
Reflections of a Transracial Adoptee [17,18]

Originally created in 1999.

In the summer of 1999, the author began a six-month, intimate and reflective exploration of her experiences. She confronted and considered potential bias by making herself as transparent as possible. The author was guided by three core questions: Do I belong? Where do I belong? How do I belong? The conclusion is that racial identity for the author is dynamic, non-static and non-hierarchical, and is defined by five constructs: genetic racial identity, imposed racial identity, cognitive racial identity, feeling racial identity and visual racial identity, captured in The Harris Racial Identity Theory.

I write this piece because I believe the evolution of my racial and cultural identity is worth capturing. It is dedicated to the scores of foster children, fellow adoptees, and mixed race persons (young and old) who silently sit alone (at work, at home, at school, or in jail) trying to make sense of who they are racially and culturally and wondering if there will ever come a time when they feel as if they belong.

---

[17] In 2008 at the 7th Annual Courage and Curiosity Celebration, the Center for Family Connections in Cambridge, Massachusetts honored this author for her pioneering work in the development of racial identity theory.

[18] See, Ung, T., Harris O'Connor, S., Pillidge, R. (2012). The development of racial identity in transracially adopted persons: An ecological approach. *Adoption and Fostering* (Fall/Winter).

Black, or part Black and part White, or Black, Indian and White, or Black with White parents, or just simply brown or basically just White are various ways in which I have been racially defined and have defined myself throughout my life.

Puerto-Rican, Cape Verdean, Jordanian, and Ethiopian are additional ethnicities that some people have questioned me to be.

Jungle bunny, bush monkey, zebra, Oreo cookie and a vanilla-filled chocolate cupcake are the animal and food categories that I have been periodically placed in.

Do you have any idea how difficult it's been to achieve a solid racial and cultural identity, particularly when you find yourself being relabeled and re-boxed into boxes that continue to get smaller? I am connected to the races but belong in total to none. The most important question becomes, can I feel good about the areas of my being that have been discarded and/or carved at by persons from both the Black and the White race, which in total sum make up almost the total sum of me?

This is My Story and Theory

The Formation of My Racial and Cultural Identity

My racial and religious identity began when I was born. At birth I was given what I consider my genetic racial identity,[19] which is Black, White and Native American Indian. I was considered to be Jewish at birth because my birth mother is a Jew.

Soon after birth, my genetic racial identity was replaced by what I call an imposed racial identity.[20] This was an inaccurate genetic racial identity that is frequently placed on mixed race persons. My imposed racial identity in 1963 at approximately five months of age was "Negroid,"[21] or what people today consider African American or Black. I got this label because of the "one drop rule" and because of the way a nurse viewed the shape of my nose, the darkness of my skin and the curly texture of my hair. I will refer to myself as being Black throughout most of

---

[19] Genetic racial identity is the biological identity immediately given to a person by their birth parents that determines racial and physical characteristics such as skin color, hair texture and phenotype.

[20] Imposed racial identity is the meaning and classification given to the genetic racial identity of the person by society, which also becomes self-imposed. The imposed racial identity can vary for the person as they move in the world. A person may have skin color and phenotype that is questionable in a society where classification is important; a person may have many varying imposed racial identities over the course of one's lifetime. For the person who doesn't know their racial birth roots, the imposed identity is much more powerful.

[21] Refer to author's narrative "Come Celebrate My First Birthday."

this paper because that was and continues to be the racial identity that is primarily imposed on me.

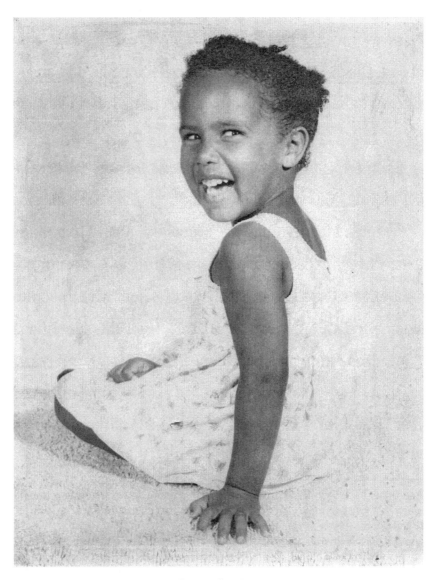

The author!

My identity prior to the age of four was strictly genetic, socially imposed and visual. I had no thoughts, feelings or say over this. I began to develop what I consider to be a cognitive racial identity[22] during my fourth year of life, meaning that I was able to hold on to the word that people used to describe me and to put meaning to that word. At this age I could associate Black with why my skin and hair were different from my White adoptive parents' and White siblings' skin and hair. And when I entered an all-White kindergarten, being Black took on an additional meaning and dimension. I saw my different hair as ugly, which led me to feel sad and shameful.

This period was also a significant time because it truly was the time when my cultural identity (which I believe is strongly connected to what I call a feeling racial identity)[23] was being shaped. I remember going to kindergarten, singing my favorite song, "The Sound of Silence," by Simon and Garfunkel. It was 1968, and the movie *The Graduate* had recently been released.

---

[22] Cognitive racial identity is what a person thinks and/or knows herself to be. Many adoptees and foster children don't know factually who their birth mothers are racially, or if they do know their birth mother's identity they may not know the racial identities of the birth father, leaving them vulnerable to an imposed racial identity. In the ideal situation, one's factual understanding of one's genetic racial identity would line-up with one's cognitive understanding of racial identity.

[23] Feeling racial identity is how one feels, racially and/or culturally, regardless of the genetic racial identity. The inner feelings do not have to match the way one looks.

My much older siblings frequently played the hit album at home. They played the music that they loved, which was significant in creating culture for me. I love listening to Joan Baez, Peter, Paul and Mary, the Rolling Stones and the Beatles. This music takes me back to my childhood, singing in the sun-lit living room, always knowing that my mother was in the kitchen, washing dirty dishes or cleaning up other messes that her husband and six children had created.

So, as early as my fourth and fifth year of life, my cultural identity was being shaped and I had thoughts and feelings about being Black. I knew I was Black because that is what I was told. It seemed quite simple. Black explained external differences.

When I was approximately six years of age, my adoptive parents gave me the choice to go to the Jewish temple they belonged to or the Black Baptist Church to meet Black children. I went to the temple initially, however I didn't feel as if I belonged. I then went to the Baptist Church and was shocked to learn that Black people actually had pretty hair. Not only did they have pretty hair, but they were also quite beautiful. I also noticed that the Sunday school teachers were nice to me, however the Black kids ignored me and made fun of me because they saw me as different. At this early age, I knew that there was nothing wrong with my family or me. Our family just looked different from same-race families.

One expert considers this time when the child is having difficulty interacting with people who look like her as a "culture shock."[24] I consider this a time when I was being bullied, and when my cognitive and feeling racial identities were being tested and at times annihilated.[25] It was also a time when my feeling racial identity became more connected to my White peers, while I was becoming further dislodged from my imposed racial identity; further dislodged from living in a brown-shelled body. And who would have known it? I functioned quite well.

I decided that I would be better off around White children who were nice to me than Black children who made fun of me, which would make sense. So I quit church. My cognitive racial identity was such that I knew that I was Black, however I was very much like my White friends. We played, we laughed, and we

---

[24] Crumbley, J. (1999). Transracial Adoption and Foster Care: Practice Issues for Professionals. *Child Welfare League of America, Inc.*, p. 15.
[25] I believe bullies, racists and bigots can exist in any ethnic/racial population and can be present in any setting.

talked. We went to Brownies and later on to Girl Scouts and Cadets. The things we talked about, the things we cared about, the music we listened to, the activities we got into, all helped to create my cultural identity.

My White friends and family loved me unconditionally even though I had hair that I viewed as ugly. I felt like I was just like them, or as much as I could be just like them, considering our hair, color, and personality differences. My cognitive racial identity continued to develop. My adoptive mother spoke to me about adoption and the racial identities of my birth parents; that my birth mother was White and my birth father was African American and Native American. This led me to focus periodically on my skin, trying to make sense of who gave me the colored skin that my adoptive parents always said was so beautiful. And furthermore, where did I get this head of hair that my adoptive parents adored yet couldn't care for? My feeling racial identity also continued to develop on an unconscious level. The people in my social environment directly influenced it. You see, although I knew I was Black or multi-racial, this didn't mean that I felt culturally Black or culturally multi-racial, even though I had attended a Black Baptist Church and had two siblings who were also transracial adoptees. I felt like I was just like my White friends and that I belonged to the culture and dominant race within my adoptive family.

I am now convinced that by the age of 7, my experience of assimilating into my family and the White community (which was positive) also laid the foundation for conflicting internal experiences that I would deal with silently for decades.

The inner conflicts look like this. I know that I'm Black yet many Blacks don't consider me Black. I know that I'm Black yet don't feel like I'm Black. I know that I'm Black, but I feel like I'm White. I know that I'm Jewish, but Jewish people sometimes laugh at me when I tell them that I'm Jewish. I've been socialized and raised by two Jewish parents and have a birth mother who is Jewish yet many people find it difficult to believe that I could be Jewish. I feel privileged like my White peers, yet experience oppression like my Black peers. I feel like I'm just like my White friends and they feel the same for me; however I am having unconscious and conscious thoughts, feelings, and experiences that are directly connected to being Black, which my loved ones don't know I'm having and will never experience themselves.

These internal conflicts were developing a side of me that none of us knew was developing. It created unknown and unconscious divides within and between my psyche and my loved ones' psyches, which created a situation where we were actually growing together and at the same time actually growing a part. I can truly understand why no one, including myself, would accurately know or understand my complete racial, cultural and religious identity. It was too much to swallow. It was too complex to understand. It was too difficult to follow. And for many, it was too non-traditional to respect.

From kindergarten straight through college I attended predominately White schools. For example, out of my high school senior class of 500 students, there were approximately five kids of color. I also belonged to a country club for years, and was the only non-White child who belonged. I never saw any other brown-skinned people on the premises. And I recall never seeing a brown-skinned person at any of the country clubs against which we competed.

So how did my social environment influence my racial and cultural identity? Between the first and the fourth grades my cognitive racial identity developed. I knew I was Black and could better make sense of why my skin tanned the way it did, and why it was light during the winter months. I was very much aware that I was the only Black female at school and that people didn't find my looks appealing.

I believe my feeling racial identity in some ways went numb. I felt connected to White people but I also felt disconnected from them. It was as if there was a film of some transparent sort that covered all of me. In retrospect, I'm sure this transparent film speaks partly to the inner conflicts previously mentioned, coupled with how soulfully and psychologically taxing it is to be continuously surrounded by White mirrors that never mirror and periodically attempt to wipe out the part of you that isn't White.

The area of me that I didn't see in the mirror (my religion, my birth parents, other transracial adoptive families, Black adults, Black girls, White teachers, and little boys who thought brown-skinned girls were smart and cute) went numb. I'm fortunate that I mastered swimming, had good family and friends, and that I had a mother who knew about institutionalized racism, and who at home insisted that I read and write.

Between the fifth and the eighth grades, my cognitive and feeling racial identity remained, for the most part, the same. My identity was very much caught up in socializing and swimming. I did my best not to feel the pain of being left out of the dating scene.

In high school, I was very popular and was quite content with myself, as I had been in previous years. I was on the tennis team, was co-captain of the swim team, and ended up the vice-president of my senior class. I also met up with the Black kids I had met in church. A few kids actually apologized for the way they had treated me. And then they did their best to teach me how to care for my hair and how to dance.

The author in her senior year after having her afro straightened/relaxed.

So how was the silent part of me doing?

My cognitive racial identity was being bombarded by various imposed racial identities. This added to my questioning and fantasizing about my genetic racial identity, particularly since I had never met or seen pictures of my birth parents. Frequently, I had to explain to others that I was Black or part Black and part White or Black with White parents. Usually, I didn't have the energy or the need to explain the Indian part of me, which at this point had been completely wiped from my racial identity. My feeling racial identity began to awaken because of my relationships with my Black friends. I became better connected to my brown exterior, yet didn't feel connected to cultural things.

During this period, jokes were made about me being Black and Jewish. And it was scary to learn that some kids actually feared that I would eventually burn in hell because I was Jewish. I think, though, what hurt me the most were the infrequent insults that came from White Jewish folks.

In college, my cognitive, feeling and imposed racial identity seemed to be in sync. I had a diverse group of friends, dated

Black men, and learned that I had experienced institutionalized racism over the years. My competitive energies were channeled into tennis and crew. One of the most significant things that happened was that I met Sidney Buxton,[26] my mentor, who is a spiritual, religious, and brilliant Black man.

A few years after entering the White workforce, I began to have racial identity problems. It was as if I had begun to unravel. I had no idea what was happening or why it was happening. I thought my parents and I had done so well dealing with racism and other life issues. My parents believed that one's backbone would get stronger, or that one's character was actually built on how effectively one could deal with difficult situations and pain. They taught me what was important to them: the physical and emotional health of their children, the finest education, human rights, an honest day of work, and stimulating conversation. They really didn't care about material things, or what the neighbors

---

[26] Sidney Buxton has mentored me since I was 18 - since my first day at Worcester State College. At a recent gathering with Sidney and his long-time friend and colleague, Dr. Kermit Crawford, Sidney recalled the first day he met my father and me. He said that my father was a smart man, a knowing man, who wanted only what was best for his daughter. Back in the day, Sidney was the assistant dean of multicultural affairs and director of the Learning Assistance Center, eventually becoming dean of academic services and freshman studies. In 1997, The Multicultural Affairs Alumni Council established the Sidney Buxton, Jr. Scholarship Award for Mr. Buxton's continuous dedication and commitment to ensure educational opportunities for minority and disadvantaged students at what is now known as Worcester State University.

thought, or even the country club scene. The country club was my thing.

So why was I having difficulty being racially different and handling racist remarks? Shouldn't I have been used to it by this point? Shouldn't it have gotten easier to deal with by now? Why was everything going right to my core? Was it because I was a person of color? Was it because I was a woman of color? Was it connected to being multi-racial? Was it because I was a Jewish multi-racial female? Did it have to do with being adopted? Did it have to do with being a Black female adoptee? None of these questions were registering, until I asked the lengthy question: Did it have to do with being a Black transracial adoptee who was raised in a White community who had been cut off from her birth history?

I believe I was beginning to unravel because I was starting to feel and see that I had been "too socialized *White* to feel *Black* and too dark-skinned to ever be accepted as *White*."[27] This realization was shattering to me. And as my identity continued to unravel, my adoptive parents became ill, and then my adoptive

---

[27] Refer to the narrative *Can You Imagine?*

68

mother died. The ground dropped from beneath me, taking all that I was and smashing it into unrecognizable pieces.[28]

The death of my mother in April 1989 triggered the search for my birth mother. I had to find her because I wasn't feeling connected to the world, never mind to myself. Another part of the trauma of losing my adoptive mother and having an adoptive father who was suffering from Alzheimer's was that I was also grieving my racial identity, as I then understood it. This insight hit me unexpectedly, and like a brick.

It was now so clear that my racial identity was very much connected to my White adoptive parents; that I had had access to things because I had White parents, not necessarily because of who I was. So what was going to happen to me now that I was parentless, now that I was a Black person standing by myself? I had always spent White money, felt the unspoken privilege of White persons. Yes, I was grieving not only my adored adoptive mother, but my adoptive father as I had known him, my unknown birth mother and my racial identity as I had known and lived it.

[28] My dear friends, Mary and Ray were my lifesavers during the worst period of my life. How fortunate I am to have such compassionate, connected and loving friends. To learn more about my friendship with Mary, please refer to our story written in *Sacred Connections: Stories of Adoption Essays* by Mary Ann Koenig (2000).

This is really the first time anyone would have known that I was having problems. What is surprising is that my visual racial identity[29] had never become distorted; meaning I always saw the color of my skin accurately.

The Reconstruction of My Racial and Cultural Identity

Finding my birth mother and her family of origin in 1990 helped tremendously with the reformation of my identity, even though it didn't stop the tremendous pain I felt from missing my adoptive mother and father. Post reunion, I felt more connected to being White, human and Jewish, and had a better understanding of my energy and physical being. My cognitive racial identity came to life in a way that it hadn't been before. In the past, I had known that I was multi-racial, but now it was much more real because I now knew my birth mother and had pictures of my birth father to prove it. My feeling racial identity was unclear. I now had had two White Jewish parents, a White Jewish birth mother

---

[29] Visual racial identity is the skin color a person actually sees. Children who are not old enough to know colors are not able to have an accurate visual racial identity. One must rule out the feeling racial identity and color blindness before determining that the individual's visual racial identity is distorted. The question becomes, does the person (who is old enough to know colors) have a visual racial identity that is distorted (which is viewed as extremely concerning) when she says 'I'm White,' when she is visibly Black, or is it that there hasn't been enough language and an adequate model to help the person express her full racial identity, i.e., *I feel white yet can see that my skin is black.*

and a birth father of color whom I hadn't met. This wasn't registering on a feeling racial identity level. Was I feeling White? Was I feeling Black? Was I feeling multi-racial? How does one feel Black? How does one feel multi-racial, particularly when White parents in a White environment have raised you? This has nothing to do with "acting" White or "denying" one's Black roots!

I was never able to meet my birth father, yet was able to meet my paternal birth aunts and other family members. My cognitive racial identity of being Black and Native American Indian became even more real than it had been when viewing pictures of my birth father. I now knew that I really, really was Black, *and* Native American Indian; that I was actually connected to Black and Seminole Indian history. My feeling racial identity was still unclear.

The feeling racial identity is the most difficult area to pin down as an adult because I am cognitively aware that behind each colored mask—White, Red, Yellow, Brown and Black, are human beings who remind me of me, my family and my childhood friends. I guess I could say that I feel Black, but what this really means is that I feel oppressed. It doesn't mean that I feel culturally Black because I am not, even though I've eaten soul food, been to Africa, have subscribed to Ebony and have dear friends who are Black. If being Black means feeling oppressed, than you could say that I am only Black. However, I know that there is more to being Black than just feeling oppressed. Another way you might look at this is to say that I know I am Black and have been oppressed like other Blacks, and yet at the same time I feel White because of my socialization. The feelings that come from being oppressed don't define my complete racial identity. Or you could view me as being Black with a "different" type of experience and culture than you would expect from a person who is viewed as "Black." Each one of these definitions, however, is still limiting, boxing me in, and lacking depth.

To have any way of understanding the essence of my complete racial, cultural and religious identity you must understand that I feel and know that I have been oppressed by both Whites and Blacks as a Black, and as a Jewish tri-racial (Black/Indian/White) transracially adopted female. Yet, like my sister, I feel I am an ethnic, non-religious, spiritual, White Jewish female—who knows

The author in Africa, after having her hair braided for 16 hours.

that she is an ethnic non-religious, spiritual, Jewish, tri-racial female who was raised in a closed adoption by highly educated, non-religious, political-activist, White Jewish parents in a predominately White non-Jewish community. This speaks to me! Yet on any day, if asked, I would tell you that I am Black or bi-racial or possibly a transracial adoptee. These categories are easy to use when interacting with people (including researchers) who need a perfectly shaped box in which to lump me in.

I love that my sister (whose husband is Black and who is the mother of two bi-racial children and two White children from a previous relationship) told me that she knows she is White yet doesn't feel White! What does this mean? Could this mean that she too has a racial identity that is layered like mine? That maybe the racial identities of our parents could have also been layered like ours? Was there a possibility that if these peculiar racial identities existed within each one of us they could have been unknowingly and beautifully intertwined all along, particularly if their identities had honored the unique and significant differences within mine?

I found it weird to feel the various transformations occur as I worked toward feeling good with living in my brown-skinned body as a self-sufficient, independent adult. And what I have come to feel and understand is that I am a human being with a backbone that couldn't be stronger. I am connected to the races and belong in total—to me, to God—and to those who love me, and accept me, for me!

"The Harris Racial Identity Theory: Reflections of a Transracial Adoptee" was presented at:

2012. Keynote/performance, Northeastern Family Institute Massachusetts, Inc. in collaboration with Parent Professional Advocacy League and Family Continuity, Annual Conference, *Getting Real About Family Voice and Choice Part 2-Diverse Family Structures.*

2012. Course presenter with child welfare expert Kim Stevens, *The Harris Autobiographical Narratives*, Rhode Island College School of Social Work Continuing Education.

2011. Office Presentation, University of New Hampshire, social constructionist, Dr. Sheila McNamee.

2011. Featured presentation, Children's Services of Roxbury, Massachusetts.

2011. Workshop presentation, ACTION/Center for Family Connections international adoption conference, Massachusetts.

2011. Workshop presentation, Adoption Community of New England, Newsletter featured the author, Massachusetts.

2011; 2010. Featured classroom presentation, Bridgewater State College, Massachusetts.

2011. Keynote performance, *American Adoption Congress Annual Conference*, Florida.

2011; 2010. Featured presentation, Boston University Medical Campus/Center for Multi-Cultural Training in Psychology.

2011; 2006; 2003; 2002; 2001. Featured presentation, Center for Family Connections with Dr. Joyce Maguire Pavao, Massachusetts.

2010. Featured presentation, Massachusetts Society for the Protection of Cruelty to Children/Adoptive Families Together, Massachusetts.

2010; 2007. Keynote performance, workshop presentations, PACT Summer Camp, California.

2008; 2000. Lecturer, Harvard Medical School conference series, Massachusetts.

2008; 2003. Featured presentation, Jewish Family Services of Metro West, Massachusetts.

2007; 2001; Featured performance, lecturer, Smith College Summer Lecture Series, Massachusetts.

2006. Workshop presentation, St. John's University Adoption Conference, New York.

2003. Workshop presentation, After Adoption and Center For Family Connections, *First International Adoption Practice Conference*, Dublin, Ireland.

2002. Featured presentation, Justice Resource Institute/Southeast, Massachusetts.

2002. Featured presentation with Tien Ung and Ray Pillidge, Massachusetts General Hospital/The Archway Interdisciplinary Adoption Study Group, led by Dr. Steven Nickman and Dr. Linda Forsythe.

2002. Keynote address, Jewish Multi-Racial Network, New York.

2002. Workshop presentation, *Child Welfare League of America Conference*, Florida.

2002; 2001. Featured presentation, A Red Thread Adoption Agency, Massachusetts.

2001. Keynote performance, Massachusetts Department of Mental Health annual conference.

2001. Keynote performance, Massachusetts Department of Youth Services, annual conference for educators.

2000. Event to feature the narratives, Casey Family Services in Portland, Maine.

2000. Keynote address, Worcester Public Schools professional development for clinical faculty, Massachusetts.

My Mind's Blue Print, Inclusive of An Oppressed Identity Construct Model: Reflections and Introspection of a Transracial Adoptee

Originally created and presented in 2010.

This is the third narrative in the author's race series. The first, "Can You Imagine?" paints a picture of what racism can look like for transracial adoptees who grow up in predominately white communities. The second narrative, "The Harris Racial Identity Theory: Reflections of a Transracial Adoptee," moves inward to explore the richness and complexity of the author. This most recent narrative was unexpected.

I thought I was done with my process on race. However, recently, I have become aware that I continue to struggle. My experience, I guess, with being a transracial adoptee is kind of comparable to (I hate to say it) peeling an onion. I peel away a layer, another layer of stuff surfaces. I suppose this is the experience of being human.

I started having this fascination with it when I began feeling controlled and annoyed by it. One day after having had approximately three long encounters with it over the course of a month or two, something clicked for me. Something that I can now understand as being a bout, or a round, or an episode caught my attention. It made me think. It made me think that maybe I was partly the problem, that maybe I didn't need to continue to experience myself as solely the victim, that maybe, just maybe, I could take control. Control of what, I wasn't sure.

Have you ever tried to examine the movements of your own cognitive and emotional experience after having been crying, feeling shamed, feeling victimized, feeling invisible? It's difficult, almost impossible, particularly if your whole being's goal is just to shed itself from holding those thoughts and feelings.

What I remember about that day was that this thing for the first time had a significant impact on me, and yet I was too emotionally drained to examine it for very long. And days later, when I went to revisit what had happened, I couldn't conjure up the events that had taken place, or what it was that I wanted to look at. Not only had I flushed the experiences from my system, I had flushed away the insights I had had about the experiences. Had I made more of this situation than I should have? Hadn't I had something legit to look at? Hadn't I?

What is it?

What is this thing that I periodically struggle with?

This thing that makes me feel insecure,

that challenges my relationships and my sense of self-worth.

Why me?

Is there something wrong with me?

Am I wrong?

Would I struggle with this if I could pass as one race?

Then where might being Jewish or female

or being an adoptee fit in?

What triggers it?

Do I?

Do you?

Is there ever a relationship between the two?

All I know is that when this thing is on,

it feels as if there's a game going on within my mind.

Being of multiple minority groups has made for an interesting existence. And the interest I currently have is looking at the movement that periodically plays out in my mind because, quite frankly, I'm sick of it. What made that day so significant is that the door to the conscious opened up. I was having an episode in the midst of feeling victimized, rather than just being a victim. This was a huge breakthrough. What that did for me in the moment was shift the power of control to me. It gave me an opportunity to look at me and at the episode, rather than focusing on perceived threats (real or imagined) and persons over whom I had no control.

Do you know people like this? People who were cheated on in the past? And even though their relationships appear to have been mended, or they have moved on, they immediately ponder whether infidelity has occurred when their significant other arrives home late? Their first thought isn't whether there had been a car accident, or that the significant other had stopped to food shop, or had merely stayed late at work.

It is how the mind wraps itself around something like infidelity, and the triggers that could be connected to it, such as arriving home late, women who present as a threat, men who present as a threat, job positions that present as a threat, that I wonder if there is a similarity in how my mind wraps itself around my vulnerable areas, which are plenty (fortunately infidelity is not one of them). I call this narrative the third in my race series, not because racism is the only issue for me in this narrative, but because if it wasn't for the existence of racism, which I believe has been my most challenging issue, I would not have been driven to write this identity construct narrative.

This is a Jewish tri-racial transracial adoptee's understanding of her mind's blueprint based on her assessment of self:

My human existence is inclusive of many significant identities. Because I can hold these identities in my thoughts, I will refer to them as existing within my mind.[30] My significant mind constructs include: human being, female, heterosexual, social worker, wife, friend, relative, social status, age group, health, and being Jewish, Black, White, Native American Indian, and a transracial adoptee.

---

[30] Note: This narrative was written in an attempt to free me from and make sense of why I was (at the time) struggling emotionally. I was deeply concerned with how I was doing. I was also cognizant from my previous works of how cathartic the process of writing narratives has been. Therefore, I set out to study the area of me, 'my mind,' that felt troubled, hoping it would ultimately assist in my healing. Subsequent to completing this self-study of my mind constructs and this narrative, I learned of Personal Construct Psychology (PCP) which was developed by American Psychologist George Kelly in 1955, from which he created the "Repertory Grid," a tool to explore how people experience their world. Refer to Kelly, G.A. *A Theory of Personality*. (1963). New York: W.W. Norton; first chapters of Kelly, G.A. (1955). *The Psychology of Personal Constructs*. New York: Norton. Kelly's main opus is in two volumes.

I have categorized my mind constructs into four groups. The first group, my *solid constructs*, I view as including: sexual orientation, social status, age group, and health. The second group, my *vulnerable constructs*, includes: race, religion and transracial adoptee, while a third group, my *bi/co-existent constructs*, includes human being and gender. The fourth group, my *role constructs*,[31] includes spouse, social worker, friend, and relative.

At this point in my life, after having done much work on myself, all of these mind constructs on most given days move around in my mind, quite comfortably. The solid, vulnerable, bi-existent and role constructs interact very well with one another.

Worth noting: My mind does not suffer from anxiety or depression, and I have never taken prescription medication, even during my worst years, following my adoptive mother's death in 1989, although I probably should have. My personality is for the most part playful, upbeat and bubbly, though intense when it pertains to topics I am passionate about. I am a people person, somewhat obsessive, compulsive, and somewhat of a

---

[31] Kelly referred to role constructs in his work.

perfectionist. I share this only to paint the backdrop in which my mind constructs move.

So, let's continue to examine these constructs as they pertain to me, within my mind and within my ecology, today.

The solid, vulnerable, bi/co-existent constructs speak to the core identities within me.

My *solid constructs* are typically quiet, calm, and serene, therefore I view them today as my privileged constructs. On their own, or with each other, they create, for the most part, no oppressive rub or friction in my mind. It is not to say that these constructs don't exist without challenge, however the challenges rarely feel as if they stem from "being wronged." There is hardly a need for my mind to contemplate how to hide, deny, minimize, or omit them in conversation unless to do so would be with the intent to avoid hurting another person's feelings. It is within these solid constructs that I realize I sit in comfort and ease, and therefore I would view these areas of my life as privileged. Yes, this is for the most part the ongoing privileged areas sitting comfortably in my mind. It is almost as if there is no need to think about their meaning or existence. They just exist, and I feel and truly believe that the environment I move within is fully accepting of them.

Although I view the *vulnerable constructs* as beautiful, they are occasionally noisy, messy, moody and colorful. They are the ones that will unexpectedly get my mind hopping when they perceive a threat or danger to their very existence. There are numerous dances or games that they will perform, depending on what they perceive to have happened, what they perceive is occurring, what they perceive as going to occur, or what their previous occurrences have been. What is difficult about their movement is that it is not confined to a particular construct or situation. When a vulnerable construct is threatened, depending on the circumstances, it can slide up to or slam into or whack another vulnerable construct or constructs, sometimes attempting to overpower or sway or take hostage the solid and the role constructs. At which point, the constructs can be at war with one another, be in agreement, or be both at once.

The *bi-existent constructs* consistently exist as both solid and vulnerable constructs. In my mind, my gender and human being constructs are very solid constructs, yet at the same time they can be very vulnerable constructs. Within my ecology, and within my mind, I am unable to say that my gender or my human being are not solid constructs, nor am I able to say my gender or my human being are not vulnerable constructs; therefore they are bi/co-existent.

My *role constructs* are positions, titles or roles I have in life. They are additional dimensions to my identity that give me purpose and meaning. With each role construct comes a relationship between me and the position, title or role, which is influenced by how it perceives *it* is being perceived by both the individual and collective members with whom it has a relationship. Meaning, this writer believes that each person brings his or her own mind's blueprint, from which it operates both consciously and unconsciously, to their perceptions and identity. The role constructs can both negatively and positively influence all of my construct categories and vice versa.

This is fascinating for me to look at. It really allows me to take an up-close look at something that has probably been playing out in some form within my mind throughout a good portion of my life. Of course, my mind has become more developed as to how it thinks and what it does, and I have more mind constructs, because fortunately, I have been able to achieve and accomplish things. However, the outside threats that I deal with as an adult are for the most part a mirror of the threats I dealt with growing up. Having been a Jewish, Black, White, Native American female, adopted across racial lines by White Jewish parents in the early 60s, and raised in a White community, and subject to ongoing skepticism from many Black Christians and Whites, really helped to carve in my mind's blueprint, my vulnerable constructs and many of my solid constructs.

My desperate need to figure out what is going on in my mind isn't because of situations that happened yesterday or last year. And it is not because I think I'm nuts or am going to need to be hospitalized or medicated at any given point; it is my attempt to make sense of and clean up a lifetime of oppressive experiences that my mind has internalized, and from which it has programmed part of its emotional, cognitive and physical responses.

My mind constructs appear to sit in a pretty solid place—which is quite frightening and rather difficult for me to say, since it doesn't always feel that way. However, I believe it to be the case. I owe this to my genetic inheritance; to the socialization, acceptance, love and support I received from my adoptive family; to having wonderful friendships during my childhood and adulthood; to having many years of therapeutic interventions; to creating five of these autobiographical narratives; to the reunion and positive relationship I have with my birth mother and her husband, my stepfather; to living without the use of alcohol or drugs; and of course to the assistance… I have received over my lifetime… from God.

It is now obvious to me that the forming of my mind constructs started way back. The following is just a taste of how I internalized my upbringing. My parents supported the growth of their six children, the first three of whom were biologically theirs, and the other three of whom were Jewish, multi-racial adoptees— two males and a female. They made it possible for each of us to pursue our dreams regardless of our race, gender, size, color or intellectual capacity. When it came to what they considered race or religious discrimination, in most situations my parents had what I consider a no tolerance policy. This is not to say that they knew how to effectively handle all situations. They didn't, nor should they have; it would be unrealistic to place such expectations on any parent, of any race. However, the significant thing is that they loved and were committed to their children, and did not turn their backs as situations occurred. They never attempted to distort my realities in an effort or need to water down or soften something that wasn't pretty. At that point in time, there was nothing considered "attractive" about being a transracial adoptive family. Out of a population of roughly 60 thousand, I knew no other.

By the time I had reached adulthood, I had experienced enough situations that were based on race, religion or adoption to clearly carve out my vulnerable constructs. Until creating this narrative, I have internalized these situations as heavy on my spirit, mood and heart. Now I am ready to further my understanding of these experiences. The following is by no means an exhaustive account of how I experience oppression, however for me, if I am able to make sense of my most challenging experiences, then I can begin to unlock the mystery of the other ones. This is the telling of my story via my mind's identity constructs.

You Are Now Entering My Mind's Blueprint.

1st Scenario: I am shopping in a clothing store, and at some point realize that I am being followed around by a white female employee who maintains a distance of roughly 20 feet. She pretends that she isn't looking at me, though I am aware that she is.

What I now understand is that the vulnerable black/race construct became quickly upset and began to have a conversation with the bi-existent human construct as to how to handle the situation. Should it embarrass her with all the other shoppers present? Should it get her boss involved and make a scene? In this situation my mind confined this incident neatly between the race construct and the human construct. And my human construct was able to quickly support the race construct in executing a plan of action that was satisfactory to both. The human construct didn't internalize the attack while it was dealing with it. It found it easy to keep it solely within the race construct. The issue was resolved, and the race construct could go back to being calm, and the human was once again left alone as it prefers to be. It loves being left alone.

2nd Scenario: I am shopping at a different store, and I realize this young man is everywhere I go.

My gender construct surfaced. "Is this guy a pervert?" it asks the human construct? The gender construct is really starting to feel uncomfortable as this man is following her around, again with that familiar distance of 20 feet. The gender says to the human, "I am really getting upset. Can't a woman shop without feeling sexually harassed? I mean we have seen this one before, haven't we?" "Oh, wait a minute! Hey, look," said the gender and human constructs to the black construct. "He seems to be talking to someone else. Oh, does he work here?! Yes, look at that. He actually works here! Do you think he was checking us out or thinking we were going to shoplift or both?" "Who knows," say the constructs, "but it better stop or we will not be coming back. Mmm... I wonder if we should just stay out of stores?"

The constructs together figured out how to handle the situation prior to leaving the store. The human construct was able to not internalize the situation however it needed to; to help both the race and the gender constructs process the situation so that they were able to be at peace again since they were feeling a little dirty. The rest of the mind constructs were okay with the way the human, gender and race constructs handled the situation. They were actually quite grateful that they hadn't been dragged into it.

3rd Scenario: I was in a meeting when my gender construct began yelling at the career/social worker and human constructs… "When we said that, why wasn't the idea acknowledged, yet later in the meeting when a man shared the same idea, the facilitator acknowledged it and went on to state what a wonderful idea it was?!"

4th Scenario: I was in a meeting when my race construct began yelling at the social worker and human constructs… "When we said that, why wasn't the idea acknowledged, yet later in the meeting when a white person shared the same idea, the facilitator acknowledged it and stated what a wonderful idea it was?!"

5th Scenario: I presented my *Racial Identity Narrative* at one of the Harvard Medical School's conference series. It would be the first of two times I was asked to present it there. What an honor. Well anyway, prior to the conference beginning, I went into the restroom where there were lots of women. I recall being at the sink washing my hands when this female psychologist who happened to be white looked over at me and apparently saw the name tag that read, "Faculty." She proceeded to ask, "Oh, are you faculty?" And I said, "Yes," and then she asked if I was there to set up the coffee and tea stand.

I mean you actually had to be there to believe it. My race construct immediately started to tick, of course and started talking to the human construct. "I'm glad we usually have breaks between these incidences." "What was that?" it said to the human construct, while pulling in the career-role construct. All three quickly responded, "She must have seen our brown skin and immediately associated brown with being a domestic worker. Isn't that fascinating?! Don't you love the fact that she is also a psychologist?! Thank God she's never been ours!" And then the social status construct chimed in and said, "I'd like to tell her that this domestic worker spent most of her childhood swimming competitively and playing tennis at a country club." Then the constructs altogether said, "This is an easy one to deal with. Let's quickly respond to what we think is an unconscious derogatory remark and let her know that we will be presenting our *Racial*

Identity Model narrative, and that she should stick around to learn something."

6th Scenario: I am hanging out drinking iced coffee with my 35-year-old white niece whom I adore... and view her as being... my... baby... when she said, out of the blue... "Aw gross...why are these people staring at your hair?!" "Oh ...who knows, just ignore it," I said. "Ya, but, when I see you, I just see you," she said. "I know, but there is nothing, really... we can do. And I am not going to put chemicals in my hair!"

The race construct then whispered to both the gender and human constructs, "Isn't it nice to have a witness, loving and connected, who validates our experience?"

7th Scenario: I am hanging out on the weekend, drinking iced coffee, window shopping with my girlfriend who happens to be white, and she says, "I've never seen someone be stared at so much; it's a little disturbing." "Oh... just ignore it," I said. "It's all about nothing. The only time we have to be worried or pay attention is if we think the stare is the prelude to a hate crime."

The race, gender and human constructs were slightly humiliated and exhausted, yet all said in unison, "It's too bad we have to talk about this with our girlfriend, but we must!"

8th Scenario: I was shopping when a white female store attendant in simple terms called me a monkey. I was in shock as I asked her to repeat herself, which she did. "What am I dealing with?" I thought, as I moved into my zone, which is rather a dissociative state that is keenly aware of her surroundings.

What I can now understand is that my mind perceived that my vulnerable race construct was under attack. And after the initial shock of the attack, I realized the race construct and the bi-existent construct of gender began having conversations, discussing whether gender had also been violated. The conversation they had went back and forth, questioning whether we looked like a monkey or a female, or a female monkey. And then the human bi-existent construct was brought in by both the race and the gender constructs, demanding that it get involved. The conversation looked something like this: "Do we look like a monkey or a human? Do we look like a female or a monkey? Do we look like a female monkey? We thought we looked like a person, but to others, do we look like a monkey?" This interaction among these three constructs instructed me to periodically look in the mirror to help obtain answers to their questions. It also got the role constructs of friend and relative involved, wanting me to get feedback from close friends and family members, just to get additional confirmation of what the constructs had originally thought, yet were currently questioning.

Once the human, race, gender, friend and relative constructs worked through the assault (which included what course of action to take) and were no longer questioning their human, female and black identity, the internal conversations died down. The female construct and the human construct would periodically take turns instructing me to look in the mirror to make sure I was looking like a female and a human. However, over time, the constructs went back to their normal state, quiet and calm, interacting with the others as if nothing had occurred. No mess and no noise: peace again. These mind constructs shook things up for a while, but the rest of the mind constructs appeared to be okay with it because, although they were not dragged into the conversations, they all knew how outrageous the situation had been – that a violation had taken place, and that space and time were needed for processing and healing.

9th Scenario: I am in a meeting with folks who all appear to be white, and the conversation easily goes on without my participation, and the human and the transracial adoptee constructs begin to holler, "Why don't you acknowledge me? I know you see me! I'm here and want to participate!" "Calm down," says the solid mental health construct as it is thrown into the conversation. "You have to stop! This is wearing, and really testing our mental health." The human and transracial adoptee constructs respond, "Do you think we want to be here? Because we don't. In fact, we can't stand this. This is humiliating! Absolutely humiliating! But we can't stop! We can't close the floodgate! You know what these people think of us! Don't you remember what it was like growing up? The teachers who wouldn't acknowledge us in class?! Don't you remember?! Don't you remember going home crying most days?! Don't you remember that it was mom who taught us how to read and write, and who boosted our self-esteem only for it to be torn down each year?! Don't you remember!?"

"Yes, I remember, but how can you apply that situation to this one? These people aren't those people," said the solid mental health construct. And that comment triggered a war, a war among the constructs, going back and forth and back and forth, pulling up any and all situations that had ever happened in the past; to the point... where it was unclear... what exactly... was being said!

And there I sat, silently fuming, finding it hard to remain there, at this point just grateful that I could exist, exist as if I wasn't there. Hoping I'd have the ability to keep my mouth shut!

••••••••••••••••••••

This is what I now understand is an example of a bout, or a round, or an episode. This is what caught my attention. When I went back to revisit what had happened days later, I couldn't conjure up the events that had taken place, or what it was that I wanted to look at. Not only had I flushed the experiences from my system, I had flushed away the few insights I had had about the experiences. I now know why this bout was so significant... because somewhere in my core... even with the war going on... I realized that no one, not one white person in that room, was guilty, of anything! This is what really caught my attention. I was having this bout, this one bout, based solely on mind-constructed triggers! How shaming! How do you explain something like this to white people who love you? How do you explain this to people who were raised and remain solidly rooted within their race, culture and faith? This is my problem!

What I can say now is that if I am heading into an episode, regardless of the reason, I am now aware that it will likely spiral into an irrational place, and it is my responsibility to do my best to leave no innocent people wondering what just happened. And that when this thing is on, if I am unable to feel cognitively and emotionally safe, the best thing for me to do is to just excuse myself from wherever I might be, because I accept that this is my issue that I must periodically deal with. And if there is ever a time that I ask for you to help (if your mind constructs will allow and are able), just listen and be supportive. There is no need to judge, or defend your race, gender, religion or stance on transracial adoption, because this really isn't what this is about... not this thing; this... is trauma-based.

So there it is. I am exhausted but that's okay, because a good chunk of work has been done. I can now go to sleep without worrying whether or not I'll be able to remember or figure out what that thing is. I now know what an episode is. I have a better understanding of what situations or series of events can trigger them, and I now know more about their narratives and the narratives that haven't yet been told.

Aren't my constructs wonderful, particularly, my race construct? She is amazing. I love her personality and how alert she is. I had no idea how busy she and the human, gender and transracial adoptee were. I mean it is obvious that they have a full-time job keeping it sane up here. This is not to minimize the activity of the constructs you haven't heard from. Like the Jewish construct, and the periodic noise that she has to tend to. Or the construct combinations and permutations of the social status, Jewish, female and the "not-so-black one" or "Black one" that get simultaneously and frequently pulled in when dealing with those who are confused, threatened, jealous or disgusted with them.

So, I am really proud of how my constructs have been able to manage it for so long. All of them have developed a wonderful sense of humor and a great working relationship. That's probably why it has worked so well for them! They allow each other to have their own thoughts and feelings about how they experience the world, even though they experience it differently. I mean, all in all, I think it is rather impressive. I really love when God steps in. He was the one who instructed me to... look... up... to figure this thing out!

Do you know what my biggest challenge is today? It is trying to figure out how to care for this new cast of characters of whom I am now conscious of. How do I do it? Do I get periodic mind massages? Do I buy each one of them a purse and a pair of new shoes? Do the ones who work the hardest get to go on more vacations, or do I treat them all the same? I'm not sure. I have a lot of new things... to think about!

Figure 1. Harris O'Connor Mind Construct Model Form[32]

The Harris Narratives

Susan Harris O'Connor

Harris O'Connor Mind Construct Model Form

Insert within calender or scheduling book to track.

Date of Situation: _____ Day: _____

Place of Incident: _____

Brief summary of uncomfortable situation: _____

_____

_____

Circle the Constructs from each category that were triggered during the situation:

List all of your constructs as you experience them.

List Core Identities on Vulnerable, Solid, Bi Co-Existent Constructs. List Roles, Titles and Positions on Role Constructs.

Vulnerable Construct(s): _____

Solid Construct(s): _____

Bi Co-existence Construct(s): _____

Role Construct(s): _____

Identified Mind Constructed Triggers: _____

Identified Assault(s): _____

Response: _____

_____

_____

Supports or comfort measures taken: _____

_____

_____

Effectiveness: _____

_____

---

[32] This form was created by the Author for herself to track and address what she now understands as being episodes.

"My Mind's Blueprint" was presented at:

2012. Keynote/performance, discussant, Dr. John Raible, St. John's University 7th Biennial Adoption Conference, New York.

2012. Keynote performance, Northeastern Family Institute Massachusetts, Inc., in collaboration with the Parent Professional Advocacy League and Family Continuity, Annual Conference, *Getting Real About Family Voice and Choice Part 2-Diverse Family Structures.*

2012, 2011, 2010. Featured presentation, Boston University Medical Campus/Center for Multicultural Training in Psychology, Massachusetts.

2012. Featured presentation, Renewal House, Massachusetts.

2012. Course presenter with child welfare expert Kim Stevens, *The Harris Autobiographical Narratives*, Rhode Island College School of Social Work Continuing Education.

2012. Selected performance, *The Alliance for the Study of Adoption and Culture* conference at Scripps College, Claremont, California.

2012. Featured presentation, Children's Services of Roxbury, Massachusetts.

2011. Office presentation, University of New Hampshire, social constructionist, Dr. Sheila McNamee.

2011. Featured performance, PACT Family Camp, California.

2011. Keynote performance, ACTION/Center for Family Connections *International Adoption Conference*, Massachusetts.

2011. Lecturer, Harvard Medical School Conference Series: *Contemporary Families/Contemporary Issues*, Massachusetts.

2011. Keynote performance, American Adoption Congress Annual Conference, Florida.

2010. Classroom presentation, Bridgewater State College School of Social Work, Massachusetts.

2010. Featured speaker, CFFC, Certification Program, Massachusetts.

Closing Remarks

I began writing and memorizing my works to compensate for challenges that I believe fall under the category of learning difficulties. The style of my writing, and the memorization of my earlier writings, allowed me to speak publicly in a way that I wished I could have done naturally; the eloquent way a lecturer speaks. Presenting these works gave me a glimpse of what it felt like to be perceived as skilled in areas where I was deficient.

These deficits, combined with the drive to contribute to the discussion around the transracial adoption experience, gave me additional gifts that cannot be seen. Each narrative I created assisted me in a healing process related to the subject matter of that narrative. The healing came, not from the writing, but from the ability to reflect for long periods of time as I emotionally worked my way through, while slowly crafting each sentence that I felt was a necessary part of a series of sentences that would tell the story. Because I had difficulty writing, it forced me to move slowly, allowing me the opportunity to emotionally and intellectually process the material. And because I write with emotion, the deficit, coupled with emotions and deep clinical understanding, assisted me in my healing. For example, my birth father narrative, the shortest narrative I present, took me nine months to write. I remember crying through at least the first six months of writing; by the time the eighth month arrived and I was still slowly writing, I couldn't wait to complete the piece, because I was emotionally done. I have not felt any sadness from not knowing my birth father since completing that narrative. The process allowed me to be completely resolved about it.

Another example of what I consider an unexpected miracle relates to my racial identity narrative. I went from not knowing how to make sense of whatever I was, to creating a model and becoming at peace with my rich, magnificent racial identity. The same miraculous situation happened for me in *Come Celebrate My First Birthday*. I no longer have the numbness that I described at the beginning of the narrative. And I now love watching parents play with their babies.

These noted miracles, received from the process of creating the narratives, are what led me to create my latest narrative, *My Mind's Blueprint*. I knew, through my previous experiences with my technique in writing narratives that I might be able to get some type of relief, possibly forever, if I could figure out why I was struggling. And so I began another in-depth study of me, and I came out on the other side. I haven't had an episode since. This is incredible for me.

I want to close by thanking you for reading *The Harris Narratives*. I hope they have given you the opportunity to see and experience the world through the eyes of a transracial adoptee.

About the Author

Susan Harris O'Connor is a writer, performer and social worker who resides in New England. She has worked in the social service sector for over twenty-five years. The first half of her career was spent as a direct care worker in various capacities eventually working her way up to supervisory and senior management positions.

Ms. Harris O'Connor writes and performs about her experiences as a transracial adoptee of African American, Seminole, and Jewish American descent. She is a graduate of Worcester State College and Boston University School of Social Work.

(Learn more at www.harrisnarratives.com)

CPSIA information can be obtained
at www.ICGtesting.com
Printed in the USA
LVOW09s2313310517
536527LV00027B/916/P